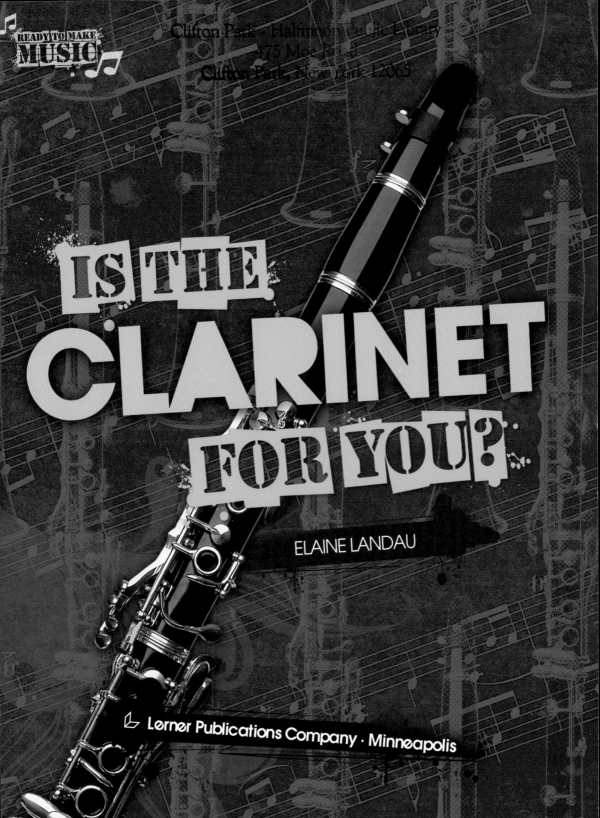

IS THE CLARINET FOR YOU?

ELAINE LANDAU

Lerner Publications Company · Minneapolis

READY TO MAKE MUSIC

Lerner Publications Company
A division of Lerner Publishing Group, Inc.
241 First Avenue North
Minneapolis, MN 55401 U.S.A.

Website address: www.lernerbooks.com

Library of Congress Cataloging-in-Publication Data

Landau, Elaine.
    Is the clarinet for you? / by Elaine Landau.
        p.   cm. — (Ready to make music)
    Includes bibliographical references and index.
    ISBN 978-0-7613-5421-5 (lib. bdg. : alk. paper
    1. Clarinet—Juvenile literature I. Title.
ML945.L36 2011
788.6'219—dc22   2009049495

Manufactured in the United States of America
1 – DP – 7/15/10

CONTENTS

CHAPTER ONE

THE CLASSY CLARINET

Picture this:

You play the clarinet with an orchestra. You've worked for years to be as good as you are. Yet tonight you feel nervous. The concert hall is filled. You're about to play a solo to a sold-out crowd.

You push away the butterflies in your stomach. You try to focus on your music. That's always worked for you before. That focus works for you tonight too. You play beautifully. The audience leaves the concert hall delighted.

Switch to this scene. You're a swinging clarinetist with a rock band. Yes, you read it right. You bring a classy touch to your band's music. Your fans love you.

When it's time for your clarinet solo, the audience goes wild. The drummer backs you up with a rocking beat. Tomorrow the music critics will call your show amazing.

Practice hard, and you just might become a master clarinetist someday.

4

Many people know the clarinet as an orchestral instrument. But it can also really rock! Here a boy plays the clarinet alongside his brother on electric guitar.

Can you see yourself in either of these scenes? The clarinet is versatile, so either scene just might be possible. But there's one thing you have to do first. You've got to learn to play the clarinet beautifully.

WHY PLAY THE CLARINET?

There are a lot of great reasons to take up the clarinet. Here are just a few. You may be able to think of even more.

EASY TO CARRY

The clarinet is not a heavy instrument. It's light enough to easily carry and comes apart into five pieces. These fit into a fairly small carrying case. You can take a clarinet with you on a school bus. It'll fit into your locker too. You can't say the same for a bass drum or a cello!

PERFECT FOR A YOUNG PERSON

The clarinet is ideal for a young person. Why? It doesn't require much breath to play. Other instruments like the trumpet or the tuba take quite a bit of air to play. Players' lungs have to be well developed. But even players who are not fully grown can usually play the clarinet.

NOT TOO COSTLY

Need to stretch your music budget? Not every family has a lot of money to spend on an instrument. The clarinet does not cost as much as some instruments. There are also ways a beginning student can cut down on the price.

Think about getting a plastic clarinet. These don't cost as much as the wooden ones. They are lighter and easier to care for too. They don't usually have the same sound quality as wooden clarinets, but they are perfect for beginners.

Student clarinets like the one this boy is playing tend not to cost too much.

THE WOODWIND FAMILY

Most people live in families of one kind or another. Family members often have a lot in common. Do people say you have your brother's laugh? Is your hair curly like your mom's? And hey—are those your uncle Charlie's freckles?

Instruments are grouped in families too. The clarinet is in the woodwind family. So what do woodwind instruments have in common? All of them are played by blowing air either over or through them. Musicians use vibrating or moving air to create all sorts of different sounds on woodwind instruments.

Can you name some other instruments in the woodwind family? The flute, the oboe, and the bassoon are a few. Check them out! All of them make very beautiful music.

A musician checks out a flute, a sax, and a clarinet. All are in the woodwind family.

Another way you can save money is by renting rather than buying a clarinet. Renting gives you a chance to try out the instrument before you buy one. You could also buy a used clarinet. Lots of these "pre-loved" instruments are still in good condition.

A REALLY PERSONAL INSTRUMENT

Do you like the idea of playing a really personal instrument? The clarinet fits the bill here too. The clarinet is silent without your breath. Many clarinet players say their instrument feels like a part of themselves. As clarinetist Iliana Rose put it, "The clarinet needs your breath, your wind. It's like you're breathing life into the instrument. It requires something deeper inside of you."

LOVE THAT CLARINET

Of course, there's really only one good reason to play the clarinet. It's because you love its sound. The clarinet can produce a broad range of notes. It can sound bright and cheerful or muted and sad.

Clarinetist Margaret Donaghue had this to say about the instrument's sound. "The clarinet's sound makes it special. You can make many different tones with a clarinet. It's sort of like a painter using different shades of the same color in a painting."

Does the clarinet's sound appeal to you? Do you love its rich and moody tone? If so, the clarinet just may be right for you.

MEET THE FLUTE

The clarinet is wonderful, but what if you're not sure it suits you? Then maybe you'll want to try the flute. This woodwind cousin of the clarinet has a clear, bright sound. It can hit those really high notes. Some say the flute's tone is light and airy.

Early flutes were mostly made of wood. But these days, flutes are usually made of metal. Some are silver, gold, or even platinum. You can see them shining brightly from the woodwind section.

Does an eye-catching, high-pitched instrument appeal to you? Then get to know the flute. It might be just your style.

THE CLARINET—A CLOSE-UP LOOK

Take a look at a clarinet. At first, it may seem like just a simple tube. But there's a lot more to a clarinet than that. Clarinets are made up of five different pieces. Each piece is important to the instrument's sound.

UPPER JOINT

The upper joint of the clarinet is between the barrel and the lower joint. The upper joint has metal keys on it. Pressing down on the keys and letting go covers and uncovers holes in the instrument. Small pads beneath the keys help prevent the air clarinetists blow into the instrument from leaking out of the holes. This lets the clarinet play a range of notes. Clarinetists work the keys on the upper joint with their left hand.

BELL

There are no bells to ring on a clarinet. Rather, *bell* is the name for the bell-shaped end of the instrument. The bell amplifies (makes louder) the clarinet's sound.

MOUTHPIECE

The clarinet's mouthpiece is at the very top of the instrument. A single wooden reed is attached to the mouthpiece. When the player blows into the mouthpiece, the reed vibrates (moves back and forth). This produces the clarinet's sound.

BARREL

The barrel is a short tube. It connects the mouthpiece to the clarinet's upper joint. Think of your own body. Your neck connects your head to the rest of your body. The barrel sort of does the same thing for the clarinet.

LOWER JOINT

The lower joint is the part of the clarinet between the upper joint and the bell at the instrument's end. The lower joint also has metal keys. Players use their right hand to work these.

CHAPTER TWO

SO MANY WAYS TO PLAY

Perhaps you like the clarinet, but you also really like rock music. You even think you might want to play in a rock band someday. Can the clarinet *really* have a place in rock and roll? You bet! No need to trade the clarinet for an electric guitar.

At times, some of the best rock bands around have used the clarinet. Its sound has made their music extra special. The Beatles used the instrument in their song "Here Comes the Sun." They also used it in "I Am the

The Beatles used the clarinet in several of their songs. Here the band performs with guitars and drums.

Walrus." And have you ever heard the Beatles' tune called "When I'm Sixty-Four"? Beatle Paul McCartney wrote it when he was just sixteen years old. A trio of clarinets was used in recording the song. McCartney insisted on using clarinets to give the piece a classical feel.

The British band Supertramp has also used the clarinet. Supertramp topped the charts in the 1970s. Supertramp hits such as "If Everyone Was Listening," "Crime of the Century," and "The Logical Song" helped introduce the clarinet to rock and pop fans.

Rock artists from Radiohead and Pink Floyd to Aerosmith and Billy Joel have used the clarinet as well. Do you think you'd like to play the clarinet in a rock band? Then listen to rock music that features the clarinet. The more you listen, the more you'll learn about how the clarinet's sound can fit with rock and roll.

John A. Helliwell of Supertramp performs on his clarinet.

QUIZ TIME!

Question: What famous California rock group used the clarinet in their groundbreaking recording called *Pet Sounds*?

Answer: The Beach Boys

   The Beach Boys released *Pet Sounds* back in 1966. The album was quite different from their previous recordings. Those albums feature songs about love and fun in the sun. *Pet Sounds* includes several serious songs. And it has a rich, symphony-like quality.
   Pet Sounds uses a number of instruments not often used in rock songs. These include flutes, bells, organs, and harpsichords. The instruments add style and flair to the album.
   Pet Sounds has become a Beach Boys classic. It's sold more than a million copies worldwide. Many music critics have called it one of the greatest albums ever made.

Brian Wilson of the Beach Boys records *Pet Sounds* in 1966.

THE PIZZAZZ OF JAZZ

Maybe you're more into jazz than rock. If playing jazz clarinet is up your alley, then you're in luck! Clarinet players have long had a place in the jazz world. Some of these clarinet players also play the sax. In jazz sax players often double on the clarinet.

Do you like Dixieland jazz? It's hard to stay in your seat when you hear that beat. Jazz clarinetists have played in Dixieland bands since this music got its start in New Orleans, Louisiana.

Jazz clarinetists also made their mark on the big band era. During the mid-1930s, clarinetists often played in jazz ensembles (groups) known as big bands. These ensembles brought in a lively style of jazz called swing. Young people loved to dance to this music. Soon swing reached the top of the music charts.

The best-known swing clarinetist was Benny Goodman. Goodman began playing in dance halls near his home in Chicago, Illinois, when he was just fourteen. Later on, he became known for the great jazz bands he put together. Goodman performed and toured for over fifty years. People call him the King of Swing.

Benny Goodman

MORE THAN ONE IS FUN!

Think all clarinets are alike? Think again. The clarinet most people know is the B-flat clarinet. That's the clarinet most often played in bands and jazz groups. Another type of clarinet is the bass clarinet. This clarinet has a deeper sound than the B-flat clarinet. It is also quite a bit larger. A third type of clarinet is the double bass clarinet. The double bass instrument has an even lower sound than the bass. And it's very large indeed. Double bass clarinets are about 6.5 feet (2 meters) long! Many other types of clarinets exist as well, such as the C clarinet and the A clarinet. But these instruments are not often used in student music groups.

The many types of clarinets include the B-flat clarinet (left) and the bass clarinet (right).

Dixieland jazz and swing music still have their share of fans. But other clarinetists have gone for a more free-flowing type of jazz. These musicians often make up parts of the music they play as they are playing it. This style of jazz is known as improvisation. It lets jazz musicians develop their own ideas musically.

Jazz clarinetist Don Byron has remarkable improvisation skills. They are clearly shown in such songs as "Homegoing," "Mainstem," and "War Dance for Wooden Indians."

Would you like to play like Don Byron? Listen to his music. Check out some Dixieland and swing artists too. See what you can learn about their styles. There's no better way to get acquainted with jazz than by hearing this great music for yourself.

PLAY THE LATIN WAY

Have you ever heard of choro music? It's a brand of Latin jazz from Brazil. Choro music first became popular in Brazil's larger cities. But before long, the whole country was moving to its beat.

Choro music is played with guitars, drums, and either a flute or a clarinet. Some say that choro music is Brazil's own form of jazz. But you don't have to be from Brazil to love it or play it!

CLASSICAL CLARINET

Maybe rock and jazz don't float your boat. Don't despair just yet. You may be a kid with classy taste. Perhaps you want to hear and play classical clarinet.

You won't have to go far to find classical clarinet music. Depending on their size, most orchestras have from two to four clarinet players. Well-known clarinetist Osmo Vänskä has played with several orchestras. He began his professional career in 1971, when he played with the Turku Philharmonic Orchestra in his native Finland. In 1977 he became a principal clarinetist in Finland's Helsinki Philharmonic Orchestra. In 2003 audiences in the United States got a chance to enjoy Vänskä's talent. He became the tenth music director of the Minnesota Orchestra.

A LITTLE BIT OF CLARINET HISTORY

The clarinet's connection to orchestras goes way back. It's been an important orchestral instrument since about the mid-1700s. Yet the specifics of the clarinet's history are a little uncertain.

Some say the clarinet got its start in ancient Egypt. There's no firm proof of that. But what we know for sure is that the clarinet came from an instrument called the *chalumeau*.

The chalumeau was played in the 1600s. In about 1690, a German named Johann Denner began to improve the instrument. Denner changed its mouthpiece and its bell. He added more keys too. This increased the instrument's range of sounds. The improved chalumeau became known as the clarinet.

Over time, more changes were made to the clarinet. It began to resemble the instrument used in modern orchestras. By the 1850s, the clarinet looked very much like it does today.

The chalumeau was the original clarinet.

Students play classical clarinet in a youth wind band.

Stanley Drucker is also an outstanding classical clarinetist. He was the principal clarinetist with the New York Philharmonic for sixty years, from 1949 to 2009. In his time with the New York Philharmonic, Drucker made a name for himself by bringing his own special style to classical pieces. He brought fun and feeling to each work he played.

Do you hope to play in an orchestra and become a famous clarinetist as Vänskä and Drucker did? If so, listen to as much classical music as you can. Pay attention to the work of different composers. Try to see some live performances as well. All these things—along with plenty of training and practice—can help you reach your goal.

LET'S TANGO!

You know the clarinet can be used to play rock, jazz, and classical music. But did you know it's also used to play the tunes people dance to when they tango? That's right—you may have heard the clarinet on TV's Dancing with the Stars!

The tango is a well-known Latin dance. And tango music has a catchy Latin beat. Most tango music features the piano, the double bass, and two violins. But it's not uncommon to hear clarinets and flutes in tango music too.

Do you love tango rhythms? Do you want to play the clarinet? Then who knows? Maybe someday you'll be playing tango music!

CHAPTER THREE

THE CLARINET AND YOU

This is an exciting time for you. You've decided to learn to play an instrument. You think you want to try the clarinet. But is that the right choice? There's no easy answer to this question. Different people choose the clarinet for different reasons.

Sometimes people choose the clarinet because someone in their family plays it. Other times, everyone in a family plays some type of instrument. The children are expected to play an instrument as well. These kids

Kids who come from musical families often play instruments themselves.

In time, you might thank your parents and teachers for making you practice your instrument.

might choose the clarinet because—well, because they feel they *have* to choose something! But in time, they just might come to love the instrument. That's how it was for clarinetist Hudi Brenman.

"My parents are both musicians," Brenman explained. "I grew up surrounded by music. Playing an instrument was never a choice for me. My parents made me do it! My father would stand there to make sure I practiced. I didn't like practicing. But I really liked spending time with my dad. A lot of other kids who started playing instruments gave up on them after a while. When they grew up, they wished they'd kept playing. I'm very lucky to have had parents who made sure I stuck with it."

In other cases, you might pick an instrument when you enter a school music program. The clarinet is a popular choice for band students.

MEET THE BASSOON

Perhaps you like the clarinet, but you wonder if a larger musical instrument might be for you. If that's the case, you might like the bassoon.

Unlike the clarinet, the bassoon has a double reed. It also has a much deeper sound. It's been compared to a foghorn. It's often used for comic or funny moments in a musical piece.

The bassoon has an unusual shape. Its body sort of folds over on itself. If you could stretch out a bassoon, it would be about 9 feet (3 m) long!

The bassoon is similar to the clarinet but longer.

Playing an instrument as part of a music program can be an excellent way to learn. It can also open the door to playing in ensembles or other special music groups when you get older.

For still other people, chance has a lot to do with why they started playing clarinet. That was the case for clarinetist Julian E. Santacoloma. The clarinet wasn't necessarily

Santacoloma's first choice—but he's glad he wound up playing it. "I grew up in a small town in Colombia where my father was the town's band director," Santacoloma explained. "He always had several instruments around the house. When I was about ten or eleven, I longed to play the saxophone. My brother wanted to play the sax too. But we only had one saxophone. My father gave it to my brother, and I got the clarinet. At first I wasn't too thrilled about what happened. I still wanted to play the saxophone. That changed over time, though. After a while, I fell in love with the clarinet's beautiful sound. Then it was the only instrument I wanted to play."

THAT SPECIAL FEELING

No matter how an instrument ends up in your life, it's important that you enjoy playing it. Feeling good about an instrument doesn't always happen right away. You might not like the way you sound at first. But through practice and hard work, your playing will improve. Over time, you might look forward to practice sessions. Clarinetist Jonatan Braithwaite looked forward to practicing when he was learning to play. "I was about eleven years old when I took up the clarinet," he remembered. "I was in middle school, and there were lots of other things to do. But I didn't have to be pushed to practice. I really liked the instrument and wanted to play it."

MEET THE OBOE

Do you long to play an unusual instrument? Then check out the oboe. This great member of the woodwind family is not very well known. Just try telling people you play it. They may wonder if they heard you right. Did you say "elbow"? Or was that "hobo"?

Yet the oboe is played in bands and orchestras everywhere. This double-reed instrument looks a lot like a clarinet. When played well, it sounds like the human voice. When played poorly, it sounds like a duck.

Margaret Donaghue felt the same way. "I started playing the clarinet in the fifth grade," she recalled. "I loved the sound of the instrument. I loved playing it too. Even then, I knew I'd have a career in music. I still feel passionate about practicing my clarinet today."

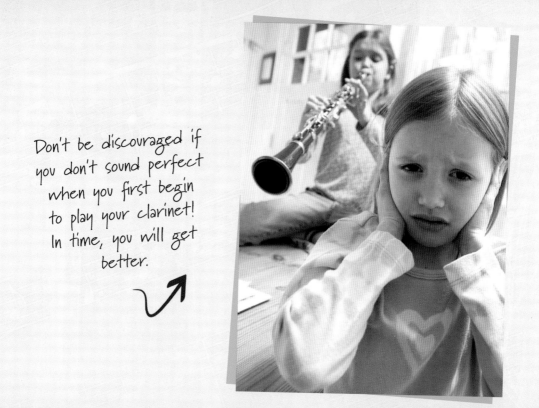

Don't be discouraged if you don't sound perfect when you first begin to play your clarinet! In time, you will get better.

TEETH AREN'T JUST FOR CHEWING

You've just lost your two front teeth. You're waiting for your permanent ones to come in. Is this a good time to take up the clarinet?

It might be wise to wait a bit. Clarinet players must control the vibration of their instrument's reed when they play. This is done with the pressure of the lips, the tongue, and the teeth. It would be tough to do without your front teeth. But that doesn't mean you have to give up on playing the clarinet. Just wait until you're a little older. Most kids are ready to start when they're about ten or eleven.

CHAPTER FOUR

BEING A CLARINET PLAYER

So now you know a little more about the clarinet. But how much do you really know? Try this quick quiz to find out.

It's smart to play the clarinet because . . .

A. It's a great-sounding instrument.

B. It can be used to play many different styles of music.

C. Kids who play a musical instrument tend to do better in school.

D. Music is a universal language. You'll be able to speak to everyone through your clarinet.

E. All of the above.

Was your answer E? If so, you're smart as well as musical. Playing the clarinet can be a big plus for anyone. But being a good clarinet player is not as easy as it may look. Keep reading to find out what it takes.

GOOD HEALTH

Think about what makes someone a good musician. Good health probably isn't the first thing that comes to mind. Yet it's vital to success in the music world. Clarinet player John Moses explained why. "Health is important in

28

anything you do," Moses said. "But it's especially important if you make your living on the stage. You've got to be at your best when you perform. Being sick can affect how you play. In some jobs, if you're sick, you can stay home until you're well. That's not the case for musicians. You can miss one performance. But what if you miss two or three concerts because you're sick? You're likely to be unemployed soon."

If you hope to be a musician, do your best to stay well. Always avoid sharing reeds with other players. This can spread germs that might make you sick. Also be sure to keep your instrument clean. The mouthpiece of your clarinet can carry illness-causing bacteria. In addition, make sure to eat the right foods and get enough sleep.

Professional musicians must stay in good health so that they don't miss performances.

PLAY NICELY WITH OTHERS

Did your mom or dad used to tell you to play nicely with others? Well, that's great advice to follow when you're playing in a band too. If you want to be in a band, treat others with respect. Don't just know your part. Try to see that everything comes together smoothly. Be on time for rehearsals, and come prepared to work. Don't demand star treatment for yourself, even if you play a lot of solos. In a band, no one musician is more important than the rest.

Being in good health will get you off to a great start. But to succeed musically will take a lot more than that. You'll also need to become an outstanding clarinet player.

GETTING TO KNOW THE CLARINET

Before you can develop your clarinet-playing skills, you have to get to know the clarinet. You'll need a little time to get used to your instrument. Clarinet player Iliana Rose described what this was like for her.

Before you play the clarinet, you have to put it together. It comes in five separate pieces. You can't make a sound until you figure out what piece goes where. That usually takes at least a few tries.

Most people who say they want to play the clarinet don't know this at first. They usually think the clarinet is made up of one or two pieces. The trumpet has just two pieces. The same is true of the saxophone. I remember being shocked the first time I opened my clarinet case. I didn't expect to find my instrument in so many small pieces.

You also have to get used to using a reed. This means putting a piece of bamboo (the reed) in your mouth. You have to wet it to make it vibrate. The first time you put the reed in your mouth, you might not like it! It tastes really weird. Of course, you get used to all this in time.

Clarinetists must put the pieces of their instrument together before they can play.

PRACTICE, PRACTICE, PRACTICE!

All musicians need to practice. There's no getting around it. Practicing is the only way to build your skills. Many music teachers say that young students should practice for about a half an hour to forty-five minutes daily. As you become more skilled, you can increase your practice time.

Other instructors feel that the amount of time you spend practicing isn't as important as making sure you play a little every day. Clarinetist Hudi Brenman agrees with these instructors. "How many hours you practice is not as important as how often you practice," Brenman said. "What if you only practice for five minutes every day? You'll still always be better than someone who practices for three hours once a week."

A music student practices under the guidance of a teacher.

"Of course," Brenman added, "I'm not saying you only need to practice for five minutes! You should practice as much as possible. It's the only way to improve!"

THE PERFECT PERFORMANCE

Let's say you know your instrument really well. You've practiced every day for months. Now you're going to be playing for an audience. You'll be performing with other musicians, but you'll be playing some solos too. You feel ready. So can you be sure that things will go perfectly?

Don't count on it. It's great to be really prepared. But sometimes things happen that you can't control. Reeds can break during performances. Musicians have slipped onstage. In some cases, they've even fallen off the stage!

Outdoor concerts can be particularly problematic. Sheet music has blown away. Music stands have tipped over. Musicians have been caught in sudden thunderstorms.

Margaret Donaghue suggests that beginning musicians learn to expect the unexpected. "You can practice hard, and then the unexpected can happen," she said. "Something you didn't plan on can distract you. Maybe you accidentally skip a line as you are reading the music. Someone can come to a performance late and make a lot of noise coming in. You may hear someone's cell phone

WHEN THE WORST THAT COULD HAPPEN . . . HAPPENS

Clarinetist Jonatan Braithwaite described an embarrassing experience he had once in an outdoor performance. "I was in a marching band," Braithwaite remembered. "We were doing a show when all of a sudden, it started to rain. A pad that covered one of the holes in my clarinet got wet and fell out. If I tried to play the instrument now, it wouldn't sound right. I didn't want the audience to know what had happened. I didn't want the band to look bad. I knew I had to fake the performance. I put the clarinet in my mouth and pretended to play the notes with my fingers. Of course, I wasn't really playing. But hopefully only the musicians around me knew that!"

Experienced musicians can handle almost any situation that arises while performing.

ringing. These sound like little things. Yet at times, they've caused musicians to ruin their performances."

"When the unexpected happens," explained Donaghue, "you have to think on your feet. Try not to let the audience know that anything is wrong. Stay focused on what you're doing. Do your best to ignore whatever is going on around you."

It's important to keep on playing. Don't stop if you make a mistake. Clarinetist John Moses compared completing a performance to running a successful race. "Even if you make a mistake, it shouldn't stop you," he stated. "It's like tripping when you're running. You get up and keep on running until you cross the finish line."

In the end, the only thing that matters is the music. Music is a wonderful gift that you can share with others. Play your clarinet beautifully and with pride. Put in the time and energy needed to be the best clarinetist you can be. If you love making music, it's well worth it. Your clarinet will bring you and those who hear you limitless joy!

QUIZ: IS THE CLARINET RIGHT FOR YOU?

Which of these statements describes you best? Please record your answers on a separate sheet of paper.

1. **If at first you don't succeed,**
   A. You try, try again. You like to finish what you start. People say you're the determined type.
   B. You feel that a lack of success means it wasn't meant to be. You prefer to try something else you may be better at.

2. **When you hear a good piece of music,**
   A. You get really into all the sounds. You feel as if you could listen to the piece forever!
   B. You think it sounds good, but you don't usually get too absorbed in it. You'd rather spend time working on art or learning new soccer moves than listening closely to music.

3. **When you look in the mirror,**
   A. You see a pearly white smile with your front teeth in place. You'd have no problem using your front teeth to help control the vibration of your clarinet's reed.
   B. All you want for Christmas is your two front teeth! You're still missing one or both of these.

4. **When you picture yourself playing an instrument in your school band,**
   A. You imagine yourself playing something small. You think petite can be neat! The tuba is not for you.
   B. You imagine yourself playing the bass drum, the cello. . . anything big! You love the sound and feel of a large musical instrument.

5. **When you think about practicing your instrument,**
   A. You get really excited. You think studying an instrument sounds like fun!
   B. You like music, but you can think of other things you'd rather do. Giving up free time to practice every day doesn't sound worth it.

Were your answers mostly A's?

If so, the clarinet may just be the right choice for you!

GLOSSARY

amplify: to make louder

barrel: a short tube that connects the clarinet's mouthpiece to its upper joint

bell: the name for the bell-shaped end of the clarinet. The bell acts to amplify the clarinet's sound.

chalumeau: an instrument from the 1600s that later became the clarinet

ensemble: a small musical group

improvisation: making up parts of the music you play while you are playing it

jazz: a form of music characterized by loose structure and improvisation

lower joint: the part of the clarinet between the upper joint and the bell. The lower joint has keys on it, which clarinetists play with their right hands.

reed: a slim piece of wood that is attached to a clarinet's mouthpiece. When a clarinet player blows into the mouthpiece, the reed vibrates, allowing the clarinet to make sounds.

solo: a musical performance in which a performer plays alone

upper joint: the part of the clarinet between the barrel and the lower joint. The upper joint has keys on it, which clarinetists press with their left hands.

woodwind family: a group of instruments that produce sound when air is blown over or through them

SOURCE NOTES

8   Iliana Rose, telephone conversation with author, July 21, 2009.

9   Margaret Donaghue, e-mail message to author, June 12, 2009.

23   Hudi Brenman, e-mail message to author, September 2, 2009.

25   Julian E. Santacoloma, telephone conversation with author, July 22, 2009.
25   Jonatan Braithwaite, telephone conversation with author, July 27, 2009.
26   Donaghue.
28-29   John Moses, telephone conversation with author, June 8, 2009.
30-31   Rose.
32-33   Brenman.
34-35   Donaghue.
34   Braithwaite.
35   Moses.

SELECTED BIBLIOGRAPHY

Brymer, Jack. *Clarinet*. London: Kahn & Averill Publications, 2001.

Hoeprich, Eric. *The Clarinet*. New Haven, CT: Yale University Press, 2008.

Pino, David. *The Clarinet and Clarinet Playing*. New York: Dover Publications, 1998.

Weisberg, Art. *The Art of Wind Playing*. Gainesville, MD: Meredith Music, 2007.

FOR MORE INFORMATION

Classics for Kids
http://www.classicsforkids.com
This terrific website includes games to help you learn more about music and rhythm. You'll also find information on woodwinds and other instruments.

Dallas Symphony Orchestra: Kids
http://www.dsokids.com
Visit this website to learn more about the clarinet and listen to the sounds it makes. Don't miss the link to fun music-related games!

Josephson, Judith Pinkerton. *Bold Composer: A Story about Ludwig van Beethoven*. Minneapolis: Millbrook Press, 2007. Josephson tells the engaging life story of Beethoven, one of the world's best-loved composers.

Kenney, Karen Latchana. *Cool Rock Music: Create and Appreciate What Makes Music Great!* Edina, MN: Abdo, 2008. This book introduces rock music and the instruments used to play it. There's also information on writing a rock song and making a rock video.

THE CLARINETISTS WHO HELPED WITH THIS BOOK

This book could not have been written without the help of these clarinetists. All provided great insights into what it is like to love and play the clarinet.

JONATAN BRAITHWAITE
Jonatan Braithwaite is a music teacher in the Miami-Dade public school system in Miami, Florida.

HUDI BRENMAN
Hudi Brenman has extensive experience in playing different styles of clarinet music. These include classical; klezmer, or Jewish folk music; avant-garde and experimental; and traditional jazz. He's played in concert halls, recording studios, and orchestra pits.

MARGARET DONAGHUE
Margaret Donaghue is a member of the Miami Chamber Ensemble and has performed recitals and given master classes at numerous universities. She is also a professor at the Frost School of Music at the University of Miami.

JOHN MOSES
John Moses, a graduate of the Juilliard School, is one of New York City's leading clarinetists. He's the first-chair clarinetist with the American Composers Orchestra, the New York Pops, the Little Orchestra Society, and the Westchester Philharmonic.

ILIANA ROSE
Iliana Rose is an accomplished clarinetist who also plays several other instruments and sings. She has composed music for films and arranged music for Latin jazz bands as well.

JULIAN E. SANTACOLOMA
Julian Santacoloma is the principal clarinetist with the Miami Symphony Orchestra.

INDEX

PHOTO ACKNOWLEDGMENTS

The images in this book are used with the permission of: © iStockphoto.com/Mark Yuill, p. 3; © Thomas Northcut/Getty Images, p. 4; © David Young-Wolff/Getty Images, p. 5; © MarioPonta/Alamy, p. 6; © iStockphoto.com/esteban mazzoncini, p. 7; © LHB Photo/ Alamy, p. 8; © Stockbyte/Getty Images, pp. 10–11; © United Artists/Photofest, p. 12; © Yves Forestier/CORBIS, p. 13; © CORBIS, pp. 14, 15; © iStockphoto.com/blaneyphoto, p. 16 (Left); © iStockphoto.com/Dennis Guillaume, p. 16 (Right); © Andrew Lepley/Redferns/Getty Images, p. 17; © Dorling Kindersley/Getty Images, p. 19; © Graham Salter/Lebrecht Music and Arts Photo Library/Alamy, p. 20; © vikiri/Shutterstock Images, p. 21; © Adrian Sherratt/Alamy, p. 22; © Richard Hutchings/Photolibrary, p. 23; © iStockphoto.com/Rodrigo Blanco, p. 24; © Anna Chelnokova/Shutterstock Images, p. 26; © Joe Polillio/Getty Images, p. 27; © Richard T. Nowitz/CORBIS, p. 29; © iStockphoto.com/James Margolis, p. 31; © Elyse Lewin/Getty Images, p. 32; © Jeff Kinsey/Shutterstock Images, p. 33; © Ferenc Szelepcsenyi/Shutterstock Images, p. 35.

Front cover: © Stockbyte/Getty Images.

APR   2011